Let's All Sing …
Songs from Disney's
HIGH SCHOOL MUSICAL 2

COLLECTION FOR YOUNG VOICES

Arranged by Tom Anderson

SONGS FROM DISNEY'S

TABLE OF CONTENTS

	PVG	Singer's Edition
All for One	4	2
Fabulous	9	6
Gotta Go My Own Way	14	10
What Time Is It	19	15
You Are the Music in Me	26	20

ISBN 978-1-4234-5589-9

Walt Disney Music Company

DISTRIBUTED BY

7777 W. BLUEMOUND RD. P.O. BOX 13819 MILWAUKEE, WI 53213

Copyright © 2008 by HAL LEONARD CORPORATION
International Copyright Secured   All Rights Reserved

Disney characters and artwork © Disney Enterprises, Inc.

For all works contained herein:
Unauthorized copying, arranging, adapting, recording or public performance is an infringement of copyright.
Infringers are liable under the law.

hese arrangements are for concert use only. The use of costumes, choreography or other elements that evoke the story or characters of a legitimate
stage musical work is prohibited in the absence of a performance license.

Visit Hal Leonard Online at
www.halleonard.com

WHAT TIME IS IT

Words and Music by MATTHEW GERRARD
and ROBBIE NEVIL
Arranged by TOM ANDERSON

Hal Leonard proudly presents
HIGH SCHOOL MUSICAL
collections arranged specifically for young voices

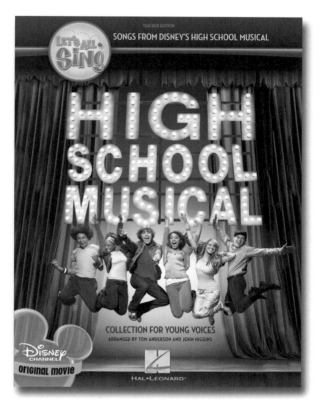

LET'S ALL SING ... SONGS FROM DISNEY'S HIGH SCHOOL MUSICAL

Arranged by Tom Anderson and John Higgins

Let's all sing, just for the fun of it! Sing-along with five of your favorite songs from Disney's smash hit movie "High School Musical" in this collection that is perfect for group singing in the classroom, community or anywhere kids get together! The songs have been carefully arranged in kid-friendly ranges for unison voices with optional harmonies. The PVG includes complete piano/vocal arrangements, and the Singer Edition offers the vocal parts. Singers of all ages will love singing along with the *hot* full performance tracks on the CD recording, or use the professionally-produced accompaniment tracks for that special moment in the spotlight!

Songs include: *Bop to the Top, Breaking Free, Get'cha Head in the Game, Start of Something New, We're All in This Together.*

09971141	Piano/Vocal/Guitar	$14.95
09971142	Singer Edition	$ 2.95
09971143	Singer Edition 10-Pak	$24.95
09971144	Performance/Accompaniment CD	$45.00

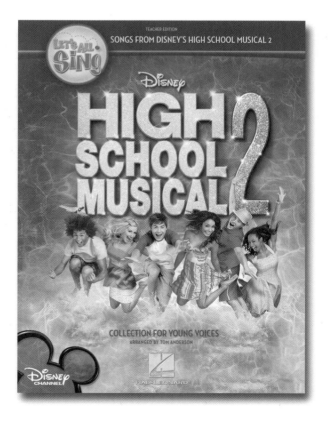

LET'S ALL SING ... SONGS FROM DISNEY'S HIGH SCHOOL MUSICAL 2

Arranged by Tom Anderson

The HSM gang is back together ... for more singing, dancing and a summer of fun in the sun! Kids of all ages will enjoy singing these 5 favorite songs from Disney's popular *High School Musical 2*! Easy-to-sing arrangements for unison singing with some optional harmonies are sure to hit the mark for group singing in the classroom, community or on stage! Fully accompanied songs are featured in the PVG, and the handy Singer Edition offers vocal parts only. Sing-along with the *hot* performance tracks on the CD recording, or perform with the professionally-orchestrated accompaniment tracks for your *fun in the sun*!

Songs include: *All for One, Fabulous, Gotta Go My Own Way, What Time Is It, You Are the Music in Me.*

09971145	Piano/Vocal/Guitar	$14.95
09971146	Singer Edition	$ 2.95
09971147	Singer Edition 10-Pak	$24.95
09971148	Performance/Accompaniment CD	$45.00